RA
Valentin

A CENTURY *of* BRADFORD

General Post Office building (St Peter's House), with Bradford Cathedral behind, May 1964. (*Mabel Bruce*)

A CENTURY *of* BRADFORD

MICHAEL BIRDSALL, GINA SZEKELY AND PETER WALKER

SUTTON PUBLISHING

First published in the United Kingdom in 2000 by
Sutton Publishing Limited · Phoenix Mill
Thrupp · Stroud · Gloucestershire · GL5 2BU

British Library Cataloguing in Publication Data
A catalogue record for this book is available from the British Library.

ISBN 0-7509-2665-1

Front endpaper: Forster Square, 1904. (*Bradford Libraries*)
Back endpaper: Modern Bradford, viewed from the university, 1986. (*BHRU*)
Half title page: The corner of Bank Street and Hustlergate, June 1964. (*Mabel Bruce*)
Title page: City Hall, seen across a yard in Union Street. Before redevelopment, the town had many such hidden corners. (*Mabel Bruce*)

Published in association with WHSmith

Public Memorial to the 56 football fans who lost their lives in the fire at Bradford City's Valley Stadium, May 1985. (*Bob Duckett*)

Typeset in 11/14pt Photina.
Typesetting and origination by
Sutton Publishing Limited.
Printed in Great Britain by
The Bath Press, Bath.

Contents

The impressive Wool Exchange, seen from the junction of Market Street and Cheapside, 14 January 1971. This building, in its heyday, was the centre of the world wool trade. (*Bradford Libraries*)

Britain: A Century of Change

Two women encumbered with gas masks go about their daily tasks during the early days of the war. (*Hulton Getty Picture Collection*)

The sixty years ending in 1900 were a period of huge transformation for Britain. Railway stations, post-and-telegraph offices, police and fire stations, gasworks and gasometers, new livestock markets and covered markets, schools, churches, football grounds, hospitals and asylums, water pumping stations and sewerage plants totally altered the urban scene, and the country's population tripled with more than seven out of ten people being born in or moving to the towns. The century that followed, leading up to the Millennium's end in 2000, was to be a period of even greater change.

When Queen Victoria died in 1901, she was measured for her coffin by her grandson Kaiser Wilhelm, the London prostitutes put on black mourning and the blinds came down in the villas and terraces spreading out from the old town centres. These centres were reachable by train and tram, by the new bicycles and still newer motor cars, were connected by the new telephone, and lit by gas or even electricity. The shops may have been full of British-made cotton and woollen clothing but the grocers and butchers were selling cheap Danish bacon, Argentinian beef, Australasian mutton and tinned or dried fish and fruit from Canada, California and South Africa. Most of these goods were carried in British-built-and-crewed ships burning Welsh steam coal.

As the first decade moved on, the Open Spaces Act meant more parks, bowling greens and cricket pitches. The First World War transformed the place of women, as they took over many men's jobs. Its other legacies were the war memorials which joined the statues of Victorian worthies in main squares round the land. After 1918 death duties and higher taxation bit hard, and a quarter of England changed hands in the space of only a few years.

The multiple shop – the chain store – appeared in the high street: Sainsburys, Maypole, Lipton's, Home & Colonial, the Fifty Shilling Tailor, Burton, Boots, W.H. Smith. The shopper was spoilt for choice, attracted by the brash fascias and advertising hoardings for national brands like Bovril, Pears Soap, and Ovaltine. Many new buildings began to be seen, such as garages, motor showrooms, picture palaces (cinemas), 'palais de dance', and ribbons of 'semis' stretched along the roads and new bypasses and onto the new estates nudging the green belts.

During the 1920s cars became more reliable and sophisticated as well as commonplace, with developments like the electric self-starter making them easier for women to drive. Who wanted to turn a crank handle in the new short skirt? This was, indeed, the electric age as much as the motor era. Trolley buses, electric trams and trains extended mass transport and electric light replaced gas in the street and the home, which itself was groomed by the vacuum cleaner.

A major jolt to the march onward and upward was administered by the Great Depression of the early 1930s. The older British industries –

textiles, shipbuilding, iron, steel, coal – were already under pressure from foreign competition when this worldwide slump arrived. Luckily there were new diversions to alleviate the misery. The 'talkies' arrived in the cinemas; more and more radios and gramophones were to be found in people's homes; there were new women's magazines, with fashion, cookery tips and problem pages; football pools; the flying feats of women pilots like Amy Johnson; the Loch Ness Monster; cheap chocolate and the drama of Edward VIII's abdication.

Things were looking up again by 1936 and new light industry was booming in the Home Counties as factories struggled to keep up with the demand for radios, radiograms, cars and electronic goods, including the first television sets. The threat from Hitler's Germany meant rearmament, particularly of the airforce, which stimulated aircraft and aero engine firms. If you were lucky and lived in the south, there was good money to be earned. A semi-detached house cost £450, a Morris Cowley £150. People may have smoked like chimneys but life expectancy, since 1918, was up by 15 years while the birth rate had almost halved.

In some ways it is the little memories that seem to linger longest from the Second World War: the kerbs painted white to show up in the

A W.H.Smith shop front in Beaconsfield, 1922.

blackout, the rattle of ack-ack shrapnel on roof tiles, sparrows killed by bomb blast. The biggest damage, apart from London, was in the south-west (Plymouth, Bristol) and the Midlands (Coventry, Birmingham). Postwar reconstruction was rooted in the Beveridge Report which set out the expectations for the Welfare State. This, together with the nationalisation of the Bank of England, coal, gas, electricity and the railways, formed the programme of the Labour government in 1945.

Children collecting aluminium to help the war effort, London, 1940s. (*IWM*)

Times were hard in the late 1940s, with rationing even more stringent than during the war. Yet this was, as has been said, 'an innocent and well-behaved era'. The first let-up came in 1951 with the Festival of Britain and there was another fillip in 1953 from the Coronation, which incidentally gave a huge boost to the spread of TV. By 1954 leisure motoring had been resumed but the Comet – Britain's best hope for taking on the American aviation industry – suffered a series of mysterious crashes. The Suez debacle of 1956 was followed by an acceleration in the withdrawal from Empire, which had begun in 1947 with the Independence of India. Consumerism was truly born with the advent of commercial TV and most homes soon boasted washing machines, fridges, electric irons and fires.

The *Lady Chatterley* obscenity trial in 1960 was something of a straw in the wind for what was to follow in that decade. A collective loss of inhibition seemed to sweep the land, as the Beatles and the Rolling Stones transformed popular music, and retailing, cinema and the theatre were revolutionised. Designers, hair-dressers, photographers and models moved into places vacated by an Establishment put to flight by the new breed of satirists spawned by *Beyond the Fringe* and *Private Eye*.

A street party to celebrate the Queen's Coronation, June 1953. (*Hulton Getty Picture Collection*)

In the 1970s Britain seems to have suffered a prolonged hangover after the excesses of the previous decade. Ulster, inflation and union troubles were not made up for by entry into the EEC, North Sea Oil, Women's Lib or, indeed, Punk Rock. Mrs Thatcher applied the corrective in the 1980s, as the country moved more and more from its old manufacturing base over to providing services, consulting, advertising, and expertise in the 'invisible' market of high finance or in IT.

The post-1945 townscape has seen changes to match those in the worlds of work, entertainment and politics. In 1952 the Clean Air Act served notice on smogs and pea-souper fogs, smuts and blackened buildings, forcing people to stop burning coal and go over to smokeless sources of heat and energy. In the same decade some of the best urban building took place in the 'new towns' like Basildon, Crawley, Stevenage and Harlow. Elsewhere open warfare was declared on slums and what was labelled inadequate, cramped, back-to-back, two-up, two-down, housing. The new 'machine for living in' was a flat in a high-rise block. The architects and planners who promoted these were in league with the traffic engineers, determined to keep the motor car moving whatever the price in multi-storey car parks, meters, traffic wardens and ring roads. The old pollutant, coal smoke, was replaced by petrol and diesel exhaust, and traffic noise.

Punk rockers demonstrate their anarchic style during the 1970s. (*Barnaby's Picture Library*)

Fast food was no longer only a pork pie in a pub or fish-and-chips. There were Indian curry houses, Chinese take-aways and American-style hamburgers, while the drinker could get away from beer in a wine bar. Under the impact of television the big Gaumonts and Odeons closed or were rebuilt as multi-screen cinemas, while the palais de dance gave way to discos and clubs.

From the late 1960s the introduction of listed buildings and conservation areas, together with the growth of preservation societies, put a brake on 'comprehensive redevelopment'. The end of the century and the start of the Third Millennium see new challenges to the health of towns and the wellbeing of the nine out of ten people who now live urban lives. The fight is on to prevent town centres from dying, as patterns of housing and shopping change, and edge-of-town supermarkets exercise the attractions of one-stop shopping. But as banks and department stores close, following the haberdashers, greengrocers, butchers and ironmongers, there are signs of new growth such as farmers' markets, and corner stores acting as pick-up points where customers collect shopping ordered on-line from web sites.

Futurologists tell us that we are in stage two of the consumer revolution: a shift from mass consumption to mass customisation driven by a

Millennium celebrations over the Thames at Westminster, New Year's Eve, 1999. (*Barnaby's Picture Library*)

desire to have things that fit us and our particular lifestyle exactly, and for better service. This must offer hope for small city-centre shop premises, as must the continued attraction of physical shopping, browsing and being part of a crowd: in a word, 'shoppertainment'. Another hopeful trend for towns is the growth in the number of young people postponing marriage and looking to live independently, alone, where there is a buzz, in 'swinging single cities'. Their's is a 'flats-and-cafés' lifestyle, in contrast to the 'family suburbs', and certainly fits in with government's aim of building 60 per cent of the huge amount of new housing needed on 'brown' sites, recycled urban land. There looks to be plenty of life in the British town yet.

Bradford: An Introduction

As you browse through this book of photographs depicting Bradford in the twentieth century, it will be difficult to imagine the rural origins of this settlement which took shape in the once verdant valley of Bradford Dale. Nevertheless, the name Bradford itself reveals this truth, coming from the 'Broad Ford', a crossing of the wide brook known as the Bradford Beck, which runs, hidden underground now, across the city centre from Thornton Road to Church Bank.

Bradford's growth until the nineteenth century had been gradual. In 1251, it was granted a market charter and in 1311, the first signs of a dynamic future trade are noted in the recorded presence of a water mill, fulling mill, and 28 houses at its centre. Although textile production maintained its presence over the following years, it wasn't until the nineteenth century that Bradford became England's fastest growing industrial town and the world centre of the worsted textile industry. In 1851 the population was 103,778; in 1801 it had been just 6,393.

By 1900 Bradford had become a thriving industrial city. Domination by the (chiefly) Nonconformist Liberals in the nineteenth century, who were largely the wealthy textile manufacturers, had resulted in a city successfully developing its resources in accordance with the latest national advances in industrial production conditions and techniques, transport and civic

Concert Hall and Promenade, Bradford Exhibition, 1904. On 4 May, the Great Bradford Exhibition was opened in Lister Park, in a ceremony performed by the Prince and Princess of Wales. The exhibition attracted nearly two and a half million visitors in the six months it was open. Among the attractions were a crystal maze, a pavilion showing products from Bradford's industries, a concert hall, and an 'imported' Somali village, complete with native Somalis. *(Bradford Libraries)*

General view of Bradford's skyline, taken from Ingleby Road, showing how much pollution Bradfordians had to endure before smoke control was introduced in the 1950s and '60s. (*BHRU*)

amenities. Bradford was incorporated in 1847 and by 1900 the Council had its own trams, electricity generating station, gas lighting, its own waterworks company with plans for a reservoir in the nearby Dales, a glorious Town Hall, Wool Exchange and unique Conditioning House which certified the weight and condition of wool. Civic pride and concern for production were backed by philanthropic ideals such as the pursuit of 'rational recreation' instead of drinking at the public house and Bradford, by 1900, had parks and grand buildings for education and entertainment such as St George's Hall, Technical College, Mechanics' Institute and Public Library and Art Gallery. All in all, as the Prince and Princess of Wales opened the great Bradford Exhibition of 1904 and the Cartwright Memorial Hall, there was cause for optimism in the years ahead for the inhabitants of the newly designated city.

Like all cities, Bradford's development in the twentieth century did not rest on local events and conditions alone. National, even global events and changes had their impact, but it is ultimately the constructive and innovative reaction to these and the pursuit of vision and the civic ideal which makes a town interesting, unique and buoyant. Bradford, to adapt a rallying call of the 1980s, is always 'bouncing back'.

At the beginning of the century, health and welfare of the many, not just the few, were causes championed by enlightened thinkers, especially in hardy working-class towns such as Bradford where poor conditions prevailed. The Manningham Mills Strike of 1891 saw the birth of the Bradford and District Labour Union, a prime mover in the formation of the Independent Labour Party and workers' rights. Thanks to the pioneering work of Margaret McMillan and later the local authority, the first school baths were opened in Bradford, the first school meals and milk for the poor became available, with regular medical inspections of schoolchildren. In 1917, the first appointment of municipal midwives was made by a local authority and in 1920, one of the first nursery schools in the UK opened. Bradford's local authority pioneered the first municipal housing, hospital, profit-making sewage works and trolley-bus service.

Both world wars had their impact on the city. In the first, the brave Bradford Pals, the 16th, 18th and 20th (Service) Battalions of the Prince of Wales Own West Yorkshire Regiment suffered terrible casualties in the battle of the Somme, while in the second, Bradford was attacked just five times by air raids with few casualties. The Second World War's greatest impact was on Bradford's textile industry. During the war, production of cloth for uniforms and parachutes had profited much of the industry around the country but to pay for the costs of war, exports had to increase and with fewer workers. In Bradford, firms merged, a trend which continued after the war was over, with the result that by 1975 fifteen firms controlled nearly half of the city's textile mills with easier access to credit and long-term investment planning. Modern management techniques were introduced and there was extensive re-equipment, 24-hour shiftwork and the effective recruitment of workers from abroad to cover the unsocial hours. Consequently, right up to the early 1970s, textiles remained a major part of the local economy. However, Bradford's adaptations could not fend off the effects of the national economic recession in the late 1970s. The city's traditional industries, textiles and engineering, shed 63,000 jobs causing unemployment to rocket to 16 per cent.

By this time, Bradford was also suffering from a poor image through negative media coverage of poor social conditions and the Yorkshire Ripper, with the

View from Central Library, showing the old Odeon cinema on Manchester Road, *c.* 1970. This is now the site of the Central Police Station. (*Bradford Libraries*)

result that the city missed out on much-needed investment which went to other West Yorkshire towns and cities. Nevertheless, boldness and innovation prevailed and the council created Britain's first Economic Development Unit which ultimately helped to attract new, inward investment and government funding. Indeed, Bradford became a successful, award-winning tourist destination. By 1984, 30,000 people a year were booking holidays in the district to sample the industrial heritage, mill shopping, literary and TV locations, national museums and the Flavours of Asia. Bradford District has a rich artistic heritage, including famous authors such as J.B. Priestley, John Braine and the Brontë sisters and Bradford-born world-famous artist, David Hockney, celebrated in the 1853 Gallery, established by Jonathan Silver in Saltaire. Drawing on such resources, Bradford became a market leader in short stay and weekend breaks and the end of the 1980s saw unemployment down to 8 per cent with investment at an all-time high.

Bradford is now a major multicultural city. After the Second World War, immigrant workers from Central and Eastern Europe, Italy and the Indian sub-continent came to work the unsocial hours of the textile trade. The largest migrant groups have been from the New Commonwealth and Pakistan. By the 1960s, they had established their own ethnic communities and by the 1980s many Asian businesses were at the heart of Bradford's rejuvenation as a tourist centre of multicultural as well as industrial heritage. The Bradford Festival, now a popular annual event, is crowned by the Mela, the largest celebration of Asian culture outside the Indian sub-continent.

Recently, Bradford launched its bid to become European City of Culture, again a bold and innovative vision for this city. Major plans are under way to extend and redevelop the 'West End' of the city, which has already been rejuvenated as a nightspot with fashionable bars and clubs around the much improved Alhambra Theatre. Little Germany has also seen extensive regeneration and is Bradford's new 'urban village'. The city's success with these ambitions will also rest on a bedrock of economic and community stability and strength, and to this end the Bradford District Community Development Strategy is well under way. Bradford is also beginning to excel in sport, with the success of the Bradford Bulls, and Bradford City gaining a place in football's top division for the first time in 77 years. Whatever the future holds, Bradford can be guaranteed to respond positively and innovatively, as it has in centuries past.

The Local Studies Library in Bradford Central Library has a large collection of photographs. We are grateful for access to those, as well as permission to use illustrations from the unique archive of the Bradford Heritage Recording Unit. This was established in 1983 to record, by taped interview and photographs, the experiences, attitudes and images of Bradford people. The photographic record of the immense changes to Bradford during the 1960s and early '70s owes much to Mabel Bruce and the Bradford Camera Club, as well as the work of Jack Booth. Many of the photographs in this book which cover that particular period were taken by them.

The photographs selected for this book consist mainly of the area covered by the city in 1900. We decided to concentrate on this in order to show, in some depth, the changes within the city, and hope that we have demonstrated these through our choice of photographs and captions.

The Start of the Century

Lister Park, 1914. On Saturdays, Sundays and Wednesdays, thousands came to the concerts at the ornamental stone bandstand. The park, one of five in the central Bradford area in 1910, also had a large botanical garden, and in 1915 a fine open-air swimming pool, the Lido, was added. After alterations in 1939 it boasted a diving stage, two water chutes, sunbathing and spectator terraces. (*Bradford Libraries*)

Bridge Street seen from the bottom of Sunbridge Road, *c.* 1900. The Mechanics' Institute buildings can be seen on the right with the corner of the Town Hall just visible beyond. St George's Hall and the Great Northern Victoria Hotel are the furthest visible buildings in this scene. Rimmington's Chemists occupied 9 and 11 Bridge Street (in the large building near left), a location they still enjoy. (*Bradford Libraries*)

Forster Square, 1903. The statue of W.E. Forster, education reformer and Bradford MP for twenty-five years, stands in its original location on the extreme right of this picture. Forster's outstretched arm, a familiar sight to many Bradfordians, would seem to be pointing to another statue, that of factory reformer Richard Oastler, which stands at the entrance to the old Midland station. By 1920, Oastler's statue was deemed to be a traffic obstruction, and it now stands in Northgate. Forster was also later removed, and now stands at the junction of Canal and Bolton Roads. (*Bradford Libraries*)

Tram crash, Church Bank, 31 July 1907. The top cover of tram no. 210 was ripped off when the car overturned following brake failure. Fourteen people were injured, including one man who had to have his left leg amputated. The driver, Joseph Dover, suffered a broken rib and severe bruising. (*Bradford Libraries*)

An invitation to Mr Cudworth (author and well-respected local historian) to join the Mayor and Mayoress for tea to celebrate the coronation of Edward VII in 1902. Elderly people were invited to such teas in schoolrooms across the city as part of the official festivities, which carried on as planned even though the actual coronation had been put back to 9 August due to the King's ill-health. (*Bradford Libraries*)

Bradford became a city in 1897, but it was ten years before it had its first Lord Mayor. Here, Bradford's mounted police form a guard of honour as Alderman Godwin is proclaimed Lord Mayor on Saturday 5 October 1907. (*Bradford Libraries*)

Bradford's fourth Lord Mayor, William Land Esq., reads out the proclamation of King George V outside the main entrance to the Town Hall, 9 May 1910. The nation was in a period of mourning following the death of Edward VII on 7 May, and the Bradford *Daily Telegraph* ran an article on 10 May entitled 'Public Mourning. What to wear and what to avoid.' It stated that for the ordinary person, the appearance of too deep mourning 'would imply an intimacy with the court, which would be in very ill taste.' (*Bradford Libraries*)

In June 1911, Bradford celebrated the coronation of King George V in lavish style. The streets and buildings in the city centre were decorated with flags and banners, and many coloured gaslamps and electric globes were used to illuminate the tower and the façade of the Town Hall. (*Bradford Libraries*)

The 'fairy fountain' and gardens in Forster Square were similarly lit up. The *Yorkshire Observer* claimed the decorations were 'among the finest in the North of England', and went on to say that they were 'on a more lavish scale than anything that has been attempted before in the city'. (*Bradford Libraries*)

The citizens of Bradford joined in the spirit of celebration with displays of their own, and a throng of sightseers gathered in Town Hall Square and Forster Square where they were entertained by both the Sowerby Bridge Brass Band and the Bradford City Police Band. (*Bradford Libraries*)

Pupils at Lorne Street School, Bowling. Saturday 22 June 1911 had been set aside by Bradford Corporation as Children's Day in connection with the coronation celebrations. In the event, rain prevented the outdoor events in Bradford's parks from taking place, so the children were kept at school where they were given a coronation tea and were visited by the bands of musicians originally booked to play in the parks. (*Bradford Libraries*)

Early municipal housing in Wigan Street, Longlands, 1967. The first schemes were carried out under the Housing of Working Classes Act 1890, followed by the acts of 1904 and 1914. In the Longlands area, two hundred and sixty dwellings in the form of three-storey buildings containing flats were begun in 1910. Between 1919 and 1939, with government subsidy under new housing legislation, the corporation built more than ten thousand homes on twenty-six estates. (*Bradford Council*)

Back-to-back housing, *c.* 1910. Scenes like this were a common sight in Bradford – middens in the back yard, cellars and little space. Concern about back-to-back housing, mainly on health grounds, was not exclusively a twentieth-century phenomenon. As early as 1860, Bradford Corporation banned their construction, only to back down five years later following fierce opposition. Much work was carried out in the twentieth century to improve living conditions in back-to-backs; where that was not possible, whole areas were completely cleared. (*BHRU*)

The Foulds family of Clayton owned and worked Fall Top quarry for many years up to about 1930. The business was started by Robert Foulds from Colne who came to Clayton in the 1820s. This photograph from the early years of the twentieth century shows Frank Foulds on the steam crane at the back, and Hartley Foulds third from the left in the front row. (*BHRU*)

Land-grabbing at Girlington, 1906. Against a backdrop of rising unemployment and a lack of government action to solve the problem, a group of men occupied land owned by the Midland Railway Company, off Whetley Lane, Girlington. The occupation took place on the morning of 24 July, and lasted until 26 October. Conditions were certainly harsh at the camp. There was very little food, and the early work carried out (tilling the soil and planting crops) was done on a diet of weak tea and bread. The prospect of facing a Bradford winter without proper shelter eventually led to the men disbanding the camp. Further experiments were carried out legally at Eccleshill and Guiseley, again with little success. (*Bradford Libraries*)

Unemployment Camp, Girlington, 1906. (*Bradford Libraries*)

TO OUR CARNIVAL
S.A. MASON.
CONFECTIONER & BRIDE CAKE MAKER
Funeral Teas & Picnic Parties Catered for

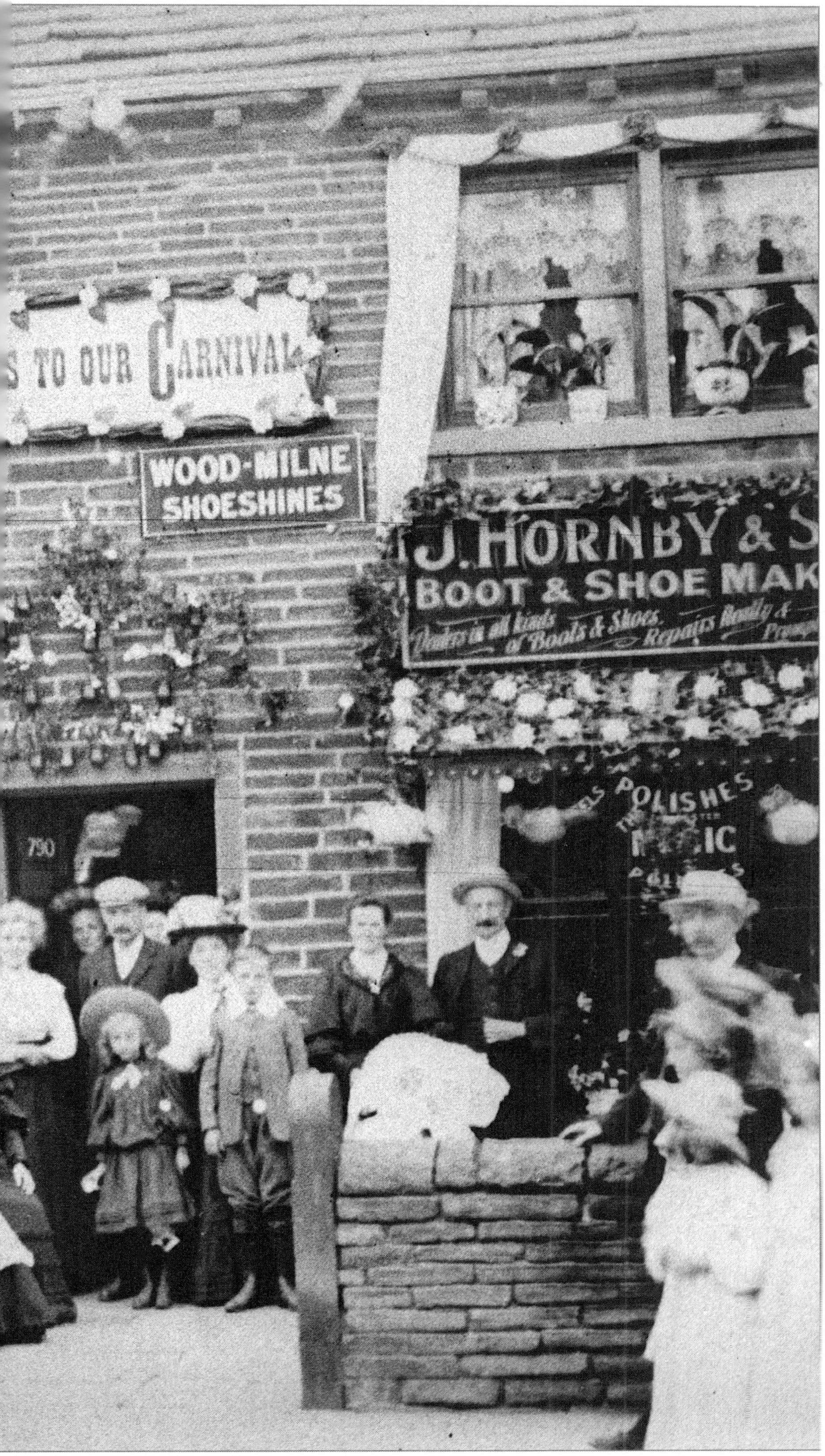

Residents of Little Horton Lane in their best clothes outside decorated shops. The occasion is the Little Horton Lane Carnival of 1907. (*BHRU*)

All the fun of the fair at Gawthorpe's Field, 1904. This photograph was taken at the Allerton Tide which was held annually during Bradford Holiday Week. In and around Bradford, local feasts or fairs held by villages, townships or small communities were referred to as 'Tides'. (*Bradford Libraries*)

Great Horton Co-operative Society's Children's Gala, Southfield Lane, 1911. The 'Co-op' was recognised by the local authority as an important factor in the domestic economy of Bradford. By the 1920s, there were forty-six branches with over 23,000 members, and capital of £477,000, part of which was used for educational and charitable purposes. (*Mr K. Thornton*)

Green Lane School kitchens, early in the twentieth century. In 1907 Bradford became the first local authority in England to provide school meals. The gymnasium at Green Lane School was converted into a large kitchen which initially served six centres. The service was extended within a year to include other centres, and breakfasts were also provided for the city's many poor children. A typical menu of the time was baked lentil savoury, green peas and bean gravy, bread, milk pudding and stewed fruit. (*Bradford Libraries*)

The food prepared at Green Lane was distributed to various schools and feeding centres across the district. (*Bradford Libraries*)

Children at White Abbey Road School sit down to a meal provided by the local authority. The children of poor families were helped greatly by the pioneering work carried out in Bradford at the turn of the century by education reformers such as Margaret McMillan. (*Bradford Libraries*)

Feeding centre for expectant and nursing mothers, *c.* 1920. Bradford Corporation earned a high reputation for looking after the health and welfare of its rising generations. The Maternity Care Committee, formed in 1914, found rooms and undertook to provide free meals for nursing and expectant mothers. The food was provided and delivered by the Health Committee. In 1921, the municipality spent £135 on food and £2,915 on milk. (*Bradford Libraries*)

Hird Lord, dairy manager, outside his residence at 167 Hollings Mount, 1908. Mr Lord built the handcart himself and pushed it through the streets delivering milk to 'delicate babies'. By the 1920s, there were 277 milk vendors in Bradford, all of whom were registered, had their premises inspected and their milk analysed and tested by the local authority. (*Bradford Libraries*)

Crowds gathered outside the popular Broomfield Public Baths, which opened on 26 June 1909. This picture, from around that time, illustrates how shawls were still worn by a large number of women. (*Bradford Libraries*)

St Luke's War Hospital, May 1918. In 1912 what was formerly a Poor Law institution (1850) was enlarged to take seven hundred beds, and during the First World War it became a military hospital. On 1 April 1920, St Luke's became the first council-owned hospital in the country. Both Poor Law and corporation patients were nursed. In 1923, records show that patients living in houses rated at £15 paid half their costs, and those living in houses rated at less than £8 had free treatment. (*BHRU*)

St Luke's War Hospital Christmas Party, 1917. *(BHRU)*

A horse-drawn appliance of the Bradford City Fire Brigade, *c.* 1905. The first motorised engine did not arrive in Bradford until 1908, so the new Central Station in Nelson Street, opened in 1902 at a cost of £30,000, incorporated stables at the rear. A system using seventy-five street fire alarm boxes was installed as the new station was being built, at a further cost of £12,000. Bradford was the first city to use such a system. *(Bradford Libraries)*

Between the Wars

An impressive view of Lister's Mill, Manningham, *c.* 1930. The 249 foot high chimney is visible from many parts of the city, and is symbolic of the vast size of the mill itself. Samuel Cunliffe Lister built the mill in order to bring together under one roof all the processes used in the spinning of silk. (*Ralph Eggar*)

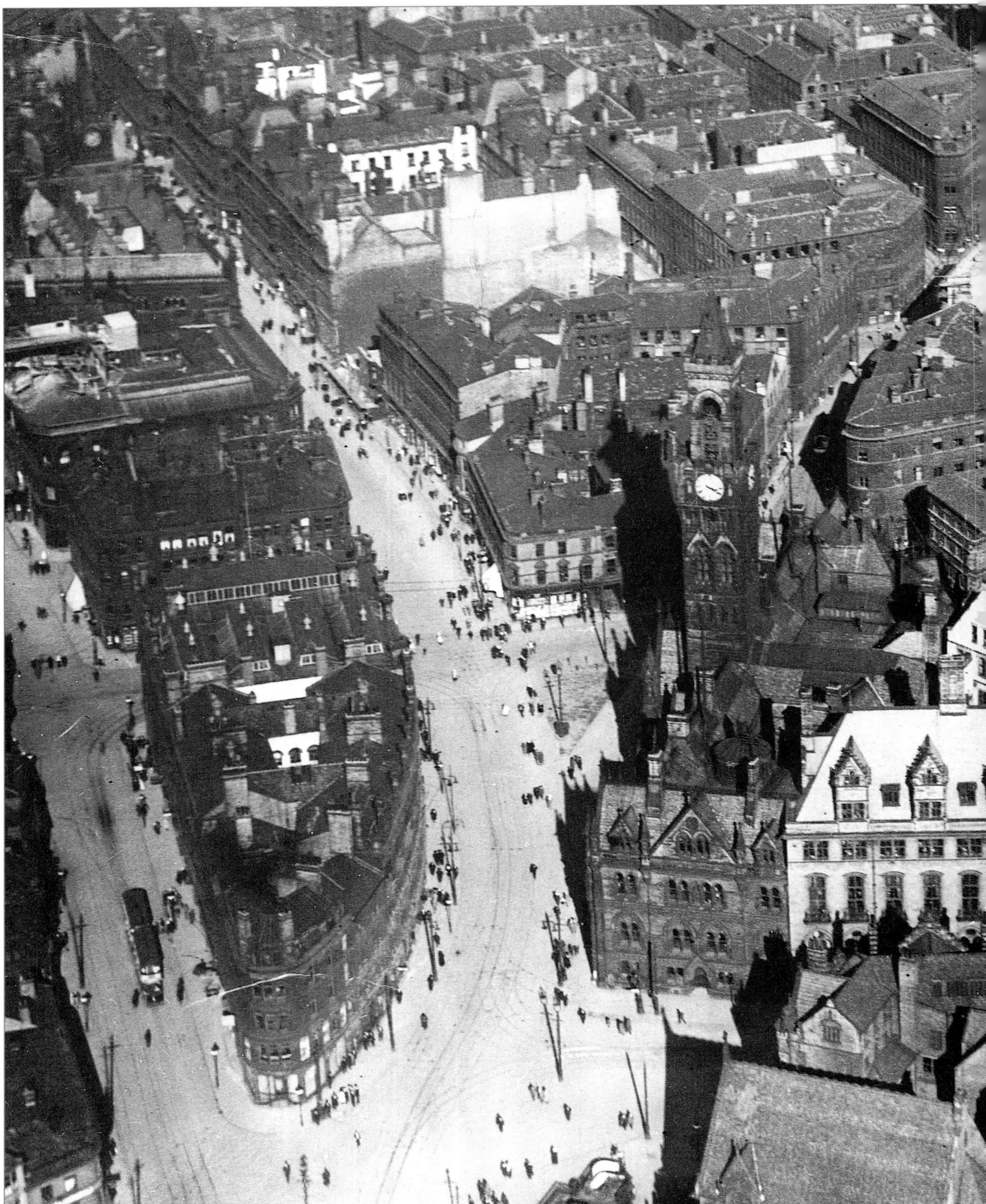

An aerial view of the city centre, 1920. The contrast between the old and the new, the grimy and the (relatively) clean is illustrated vividly by the Town Hall. The original buildings and clock tower to the left have been blackened by nearly fifty years of mill chimney smoke, while the extension opened in 1909 remains relatively clean. The problem of air pollution in Bradford had long caused concern, and had been partially addressed by the setting up of 'smokeless zones' across the district. The passing of the Clean Air Act of 1956 helped put an end to the 'smogs' that older generations will no doubt remember. (*Bradford Libraries*)

The East Bowling Socialist Sunday School Whit-Treat, 9 June 1919. Socialist Sunday Schools were formed by the Bradford Labour Church with the initial aim of educating children in the moral values of socialism, although they quickly became involved in sports galas, fairs and the like. (*Bradford Libraries*)

East Bowling Independent Labour Party Club: the winning dominoes team with their trophy, *c.* 1920. (*Bradford Libraries*)

All dressed up and ready to go. Bradford folk in their Sunday best embarking on a charabanc trip, *c.* 1920. Such trips were hugely popular in the early decades of the twentieth century. The 1920 *Post Office Directory* lists twenty-seven different motor charabanc proprietors in Bradford. (*Bradford Libraries*)

'Shout, lads, if you see any lasses on the horizon.' Outside the Crown Hotel, and another charabanc trip, *c.* 1920. Strictly men only this time. (*Bradford Libraries*)

Carding engines at Robert Jowitt's in the 1920s. This photograph shows the feeding end of the machines which disentangled, cleared and mixed the fibres to produce a continuous sliver suitable for further processing. (*BHRU*)

Delivery end of the carding engines, Robert Jowitt's, 1920s. At that time Bradford still stood proudly at the head of the world production of spun worsted yarns and the production of fabric containing worsted. In fact, Bradford mills were producing more tops, yarn and pieces than the home market could cope with, so an important feature of the city's trade was exports to the continent and further afield. (*BHRU*)

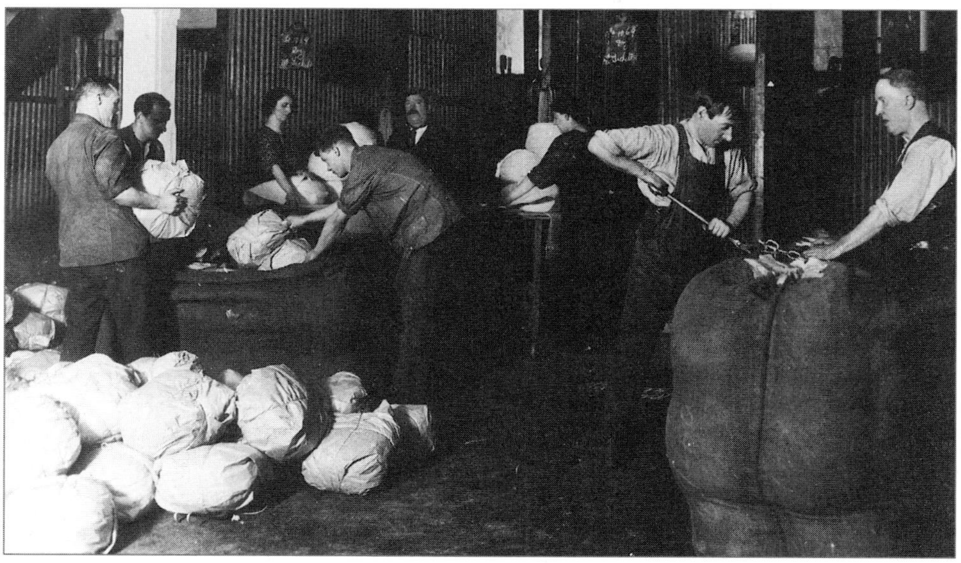

Packing for despatch: Robert Jowitt's in the 1920s. (*BHRU*)

John Street Open Air Market was opened in 1930 and in 1937 was reportedly open on Thursday, Friday and Saturday each week 'for the sale of all kinds of marketable articles and of live poultry, pigeons, rabbits, eggs, provisions and miscellaneous goods'. (*Bradford Official Handbook, 1937*)

The John Street Market stall of G.W. and M. Kimber, herbalists, who traded in the late 1930s. (*Bradford Libraries*)

High fashion 1930s style, at this stall in Kirkgate Market! Betty Stead ran her 'fancy drapery' stall at the market from 1903 until the early 1930s. (*BHRU*)

A baker's shop, Mount Street, off Leeds Road, 1924. In the days before supermarkets, general car-ownership and out-of-town developments, corner shops such as these were the lifeblood of communities. (*BHRU*)

Darley Street long before pedestrianisation. In the late 1920s this busy street boasted the usual range of shops (drapers, chemists, shoe shops, etc.), as well as a cinema, public library and market hall. (*Bradford Libraries*)

The Municipal Milk Depot, Morley Street, 1923. Bradford Corporation recognised the importance of milk as a food, and established the depot where milk purchased from 'trustworthy sources' was cooled, purified, bottled and sold to the public at market prices. (*Texture of Welfare*)

In 1920, St Anne's Nursery was opened and became one of the first nursery schools in the United Kingdom. This is Lilycroft Nursery, one of three nursery schools, and among twenty-four established nursery classes, with seven more on the way by 1970. Because of its large immigrant population and the presence of large industries, Bradford qualified for additional nursery units through the government's Urban Aid Programme in 1969. (*BHRU*)

KV 6237

Royalty visits Bradford, c. 1930. Edward, Prince of Wales, inspects a parade of old soldiers. (*Bradford Libraries*)

Looking as though they would be more at home on the mean streets of Chicago, this mob of likely lads is gathered outside Whitehead's shop, 3 Linton Street, Ripleyville, 1928. (*BHRU*)

Nelson Street Central Fire Station, *c.* 1922. This photograph suggests that the attraction of firemen to some young ladies is nothing new! (*Bradford Libraries*)

Motor car AK2, which was owned by C.H. Lord of Bradford, was entered in the London to Brighton run of 1936, driven by Albert House Jnr. His father Albert House Snr was a pioneer of motor transport in Bradford, driving the city's first motor wagonette and holding the omnibus licence 'No.1' which he believed to be the first issued in England. (*Bradford Libraries*)

A nostalgic look at two pollution-free forms of transport, 1934. Horse-drawn trams first operated in Bradford from February 1882, and by 1900 work was under way all over the city to provide an electric tram service, which was to last until May 1950. Trolleybuses ran in the city from 1911 until 24 March 1972 (the last public service trolleybus service in Britain). Here, trolleybus no. 600, which was in service between November 1934 and December 1959, passes tram no. 211, built in 1904 and withdrawn in 1938. (*Bradford Libraries*)

Even back in 1921, mineral water was available to the public. The mineral water firm Camwal supplied artesian well water to His Majesty's Government. (*Bradford Libraries*)

Coal merchant Bentley Brear and Sons, *c.* 1937. Trade directories show that Mr Brear started as a grocer of Hill Top, Low Moor, in about 1914. He became a coal merchant around 1936. The family-run business continued well into the 1980s. (*Bradford Libraries*)

Bradford city centre, looking west, 1926. This picture, taken from the Town Hall tower, clearly shows the effect of the General Strike which was in force at the time, as none of the chimneys are smoking. In fact, coal was in such short supply during this period that locals were reduced to searching the disused coal mines of the area, in the hope of finding leftovers. (*Bradford Libraries*)

An unusual view of the junction of Sunbridge Road and Tyrrel Street, taken from the roof of Brown and Muff's, 8 August 1934. On the right of the picture is the Prudential Assurance Building, a rare example of a red-brick building in the centre of Bradford. (*House of Fraser*)

A Bradford Corporation tram, decorated for the Silver Jubilee of King George V in 1935. Bradford joined in the national celebrations with many civic events, including the lighting of beacons across the city. The torches used to fire the beacons had been lit on the Town Hall steps by the Lord Mayor, Alderman Walter Hodgson, and carried to their destinations by teams of Boy Scouts. The Lord Mayor then travelled up to Thornton in time to meet the Scouts and light one of the beacons himself. (*Bradford Libraries*)

Weaving shed celebrations for the coronation, 1937. The wool textile industry had the enormous task of clothing the British armed forces through two great wars. Bradford's contribution was a fine one but, like many other cities, it faced a growing shortage of labour as the war progressed and many thousands of women transferred from the mills to either the Women's Auxiliary Services or to munitions work. (*BHRU*)

The Second World War and the Postwar Period

Workers leaving a Bradford mill, 1950s. In 1955 it was reported that besides the shorter working week, the operatives enjoyed a guaranteed week of 75 per cent and, from 1953, a fortnight's annual holiday. For a forty-five hour week, the average wage for a woolsorter was £10 11s, for a spinner £4 5s and for a weaver £4 10s–£6. (*BHRU*)

Bradford played its part in the Second World War like other towns and cities. The city recruited for Air Raid Wardens. Here, Alderman M.F. Titterington speaks about the job in hand. To his left is the city's chief information officer, Mr R.W. Parsons. (*Bradford Libraries*)

ARP and Red Cross volunteers, August 1940. (*Bradford Libraries*)

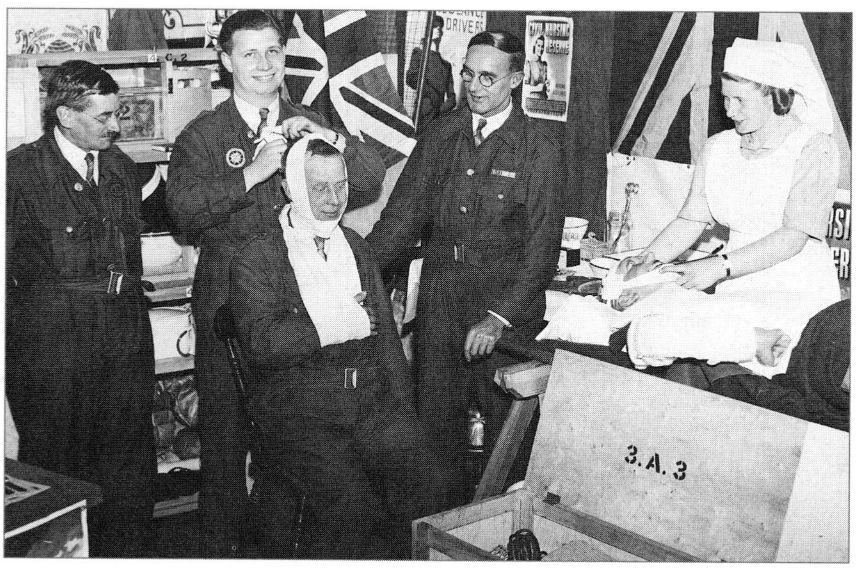

First aid training in Bradford during the Second World War. The city authorities considered Bradford a significant target for air raids and allocated two thousand spaces at Bowling and Scholemoor Cemeteries for potential casualties. In the event, the city suffered only five attacks, the worst being on 31 August 1940, when one person was killed, over a hundred were injured and sixty families were left homeless. (*Bradford Libraries*)

A display of military clothing and equipment in Forster Square Station, *c.* 1942. The display was sponsored by Brown and Muff's department store and seems to depict what living conditions were like in soldiers' huts. (*House of Fraser*)

Soldiers on leave browse through Valentine's Day cards at Brown and Muff's. Notice the ink jars on the counter – presumably one could purchase a card and write it out straight away. (*House of Fraser*)

H.R Jackson
CHINA
SAXONE

Torrential rain hit Bradford on the morning of 20 September 1946. In the half hour after 7.45 a.m., almost 2 inches of rain fell, causing the city's worst ever recorded flood. The Bradford Beck quickly overflowed and the entire city centre was submerged, causing £1 million damage. (*Mr Mullinder*)

Stranded! Members of the public take refuge from the floodwaters opposite the Town Hall. (*Mr Mullinder*)

The advertisement for dog racing, to the left of this scene, offers 'the finest racing on the finest track in the north'. Perhaps fishing would be more appropriate on a day like this! (*Mr Mullinder*)

Brown, Muff and Co., *c.* 1959. This was one of the largest and most popular shops to originate in Bradford, situated at the corner of Ivegate and Market Street. Always a forward-thinking company, in December 1927 the fourth floor was used as a 'baby park' to help mothers on their shopping trips, and for a 'book exhibition' in 1937, where there were author talks each afternoon. Authors included Margaret Lane, Fleet Street's first woman Special Correspondent, and the royal biographer Hector Bolitho. (*House of Fraser*)

The new coffee bar in Brown, Muff's, *c.* 1950; despite appearances it was always a popular meeting place! (*House of Fraser*)

Beauty department, Brown, Muff's, *c.* 1950. Earlier, in 1927, the first beauty salon with separate, fully equipped parlours was opened. In 1929 the company won its first national window display competition for a display of permanent waving, with an award of £50. (*House of Fraser*)

The smoking room, Brown, Muff and Co., *c.* 1950. The company was well known for its good working conditions and advanced attitude towards training. Many of the staff were happily employed there and stayed until their retirement. (*House of Fraser*)

In 1946 the 'retail markets' of Bradford consisted of three market halls with interior shops and one open market. In 1947, despite limited supplies, there were no stalls available for rent in Kirkgate Market. This stall shows the continued importance of canned and dried produce but the end of the war heralded a flood of demand for goods from all over the world. By 1964 retail prices were double what they had been in 1945. (*Bradford Libraries*)

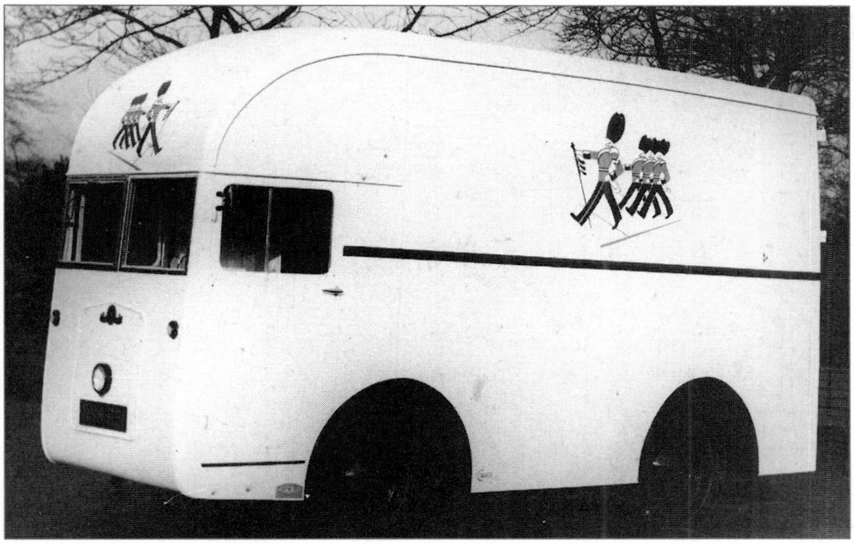

Busbys electric van, 1947. An environmentally friendly way of delivering goods! (*BHRU*)

'The Store with the Friendly Welcome.' Busbys main store, Manningham Lane, 1954. Busbys was a name known to generations of Bradfordians. The first shop opened in 1908 and the premises pictured were acquired in 1930. Debenhams bought the store in 1958, keeping the Busby name until its closure in 1978. The building was sadly destroyed by a huge fire on 19 August 1979, and the site is now occupied by a retail park. (*Bradford Libraries*)

Civic Service and street parade, *c.* 1942. This Second World War parade was taken on Market Street, Thornton. (*Bradford Libraries*)

Alderman C. Barnett, Alderman K. Chambers and R.W. Parsons, city librarian, prepare for Bradford's centenary celebrations. Bradford received its charter in 1847 and the celebrations came to a close with a grand pageant in Peel Park. Public support was lacking though and the event was a financial disaster. (*Bradford Libraries*)

Coronation decorations and procession for Queen Elizabeth II, 1953. The Lord Mayor, Councillor Angus Crowther, and Members of the Council attended an open air service on the Broadway car park on the afternoon of Sunday 31 May, following it with a parade around the city centre. They are seen here on Broadway. (*Bradford Libraries*)

Town Hall Square showing the decorations for the coronation, 1953. Many streets within a radius of half a mile of the Town Hall were decorated by the Department of the City Engineer and Surveyor, and hopes were expressed that businesses and residents would follow the Council's lead. (*Bradford Libraries*)

Town Hall Square, 1953. (*Bradford Libraries*)

Valley Power Station, *c.* 1950. In 1889 Bradford became the first local authority in the country to provide a supply of electricity for general purposes, having a grand total of seventy-three consumers! Valley Power Station was opened in 1897 and added to in 1903. Two further extensions took place in 1946 and 1948 at a cost of £1.45 million. The plant was closed down in 1976 and slowly demolished. The chimney (incredibly 50 feet taller than Lister's Mill chimney) was felled in January 1980. (*J. Dickinson*)

Looking down Morley Street, 1954. The Windsor Baths on the left were closed in 1983 after ninety years of use. Morley Street is now at the heart of a regenerated 'West End', with pubs, restaurants and nightclubs galore. (*Mabel Bruce*)

Horton Lane Congregational Church, *c.* 1954. Known for many years as Bradford's Cathedral of Nonconformity, the building towered over Queen Victoria's statue at the bottom of Little Horton Lane. Built in 1863 as a result of the missionary fervour of the 'Horton Laners', it fell into decline when the city expanded and many worshippers moved to outlying districts. It was put up for sale in 1952 and demolished in 1956. Even the graveyard had to be cleared. There are now plans to build a multi-million-pound entertainment centre on the site. (*Bradford Libraries*)

A Ukrainian protest march against Russian oppression, Sunbridge Road, late 1950s. About thirty Ukrainians settled in the city after the Second World War. More soon followed and by the late 1980s the community numbered over 2,000. (*Bradford Libraries*)

Bedroom at Lower Mount Hostel for Italian female immigrant textile workers, 1950s. Bradford's postwar effort to increase production of wool textiles led to the absorption of many European volunteer workers. In 1952, there were reported to be about 3,000 such workers in local mills. Other workers were recruited from areas such as South Yorkshire and transported daily to and from work. (*BHRU*)

The end of an era, 6 May 1950. Bradford's last tram, car no. 104, decorated for the occasion, outside Thornbury Works. The car ended up being used as a scoreboard at Odsal Stadium, before being restored by enthusiasts. It is now housed at Bradford Industrial Museum. (*Bradford Libraries*)

Buses bound for Halifax, Leeds and Baildon wait at Chester Street Bus Station, 1954. This bus station was in use until 1977 when the new Transport Interchange opened. (*Bradford Libraries*)

In 1952, the year of this photograph, there were three full-time fire stations in Bradford (Odsal, Idle and Nelson Street – the latter seen here) and a fire engine could reach any part of the city within approximately five minutes. (*Bradford Council*)

Some of Bradford's ambulance fleet garaged at the Sugden Street HQ, *c.* 1946. A centralised ambulance service was introduced in April of that year, with ten vehicles taken over from the Municipal Hospitals, Police, Social Welfare Department and Civil Defence. With the exception of Bradford's patients going into a municipal hospital, a charge of ten shillings was made for a journey. (*BHRU*)

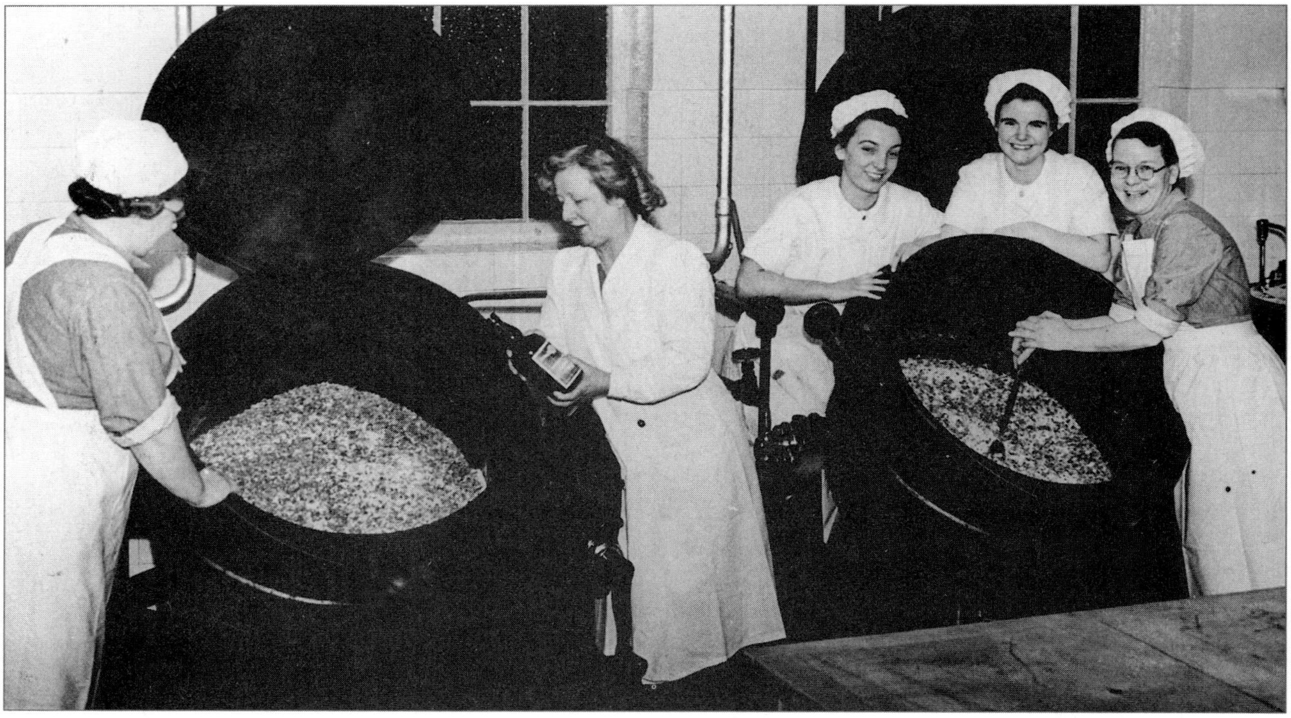

St Luke's Hospital, 1950. Staff are mixing the Christmas pudding in large boilers, with a dash of tonic wine! Another cause for celebration had been the introduction of penicillin at the end of the Second World War. BHRU interviewees noted the joyful reception of nurses in Bradford to this wonder cure. (*BHRU*)

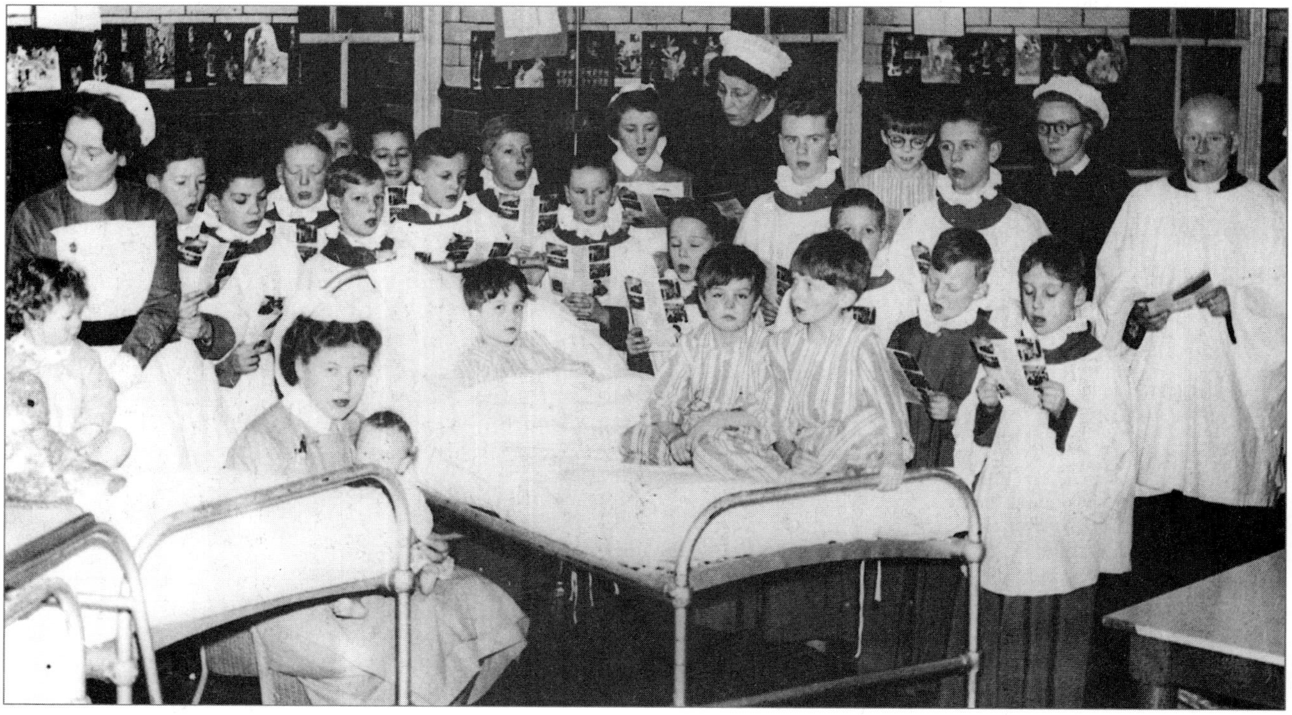

'Now when you were on a children's ward at night, you do Father Christmas . . . and it was lovely when I did that . . . they all got a little gift and you put it at the bottom of the bed . . . it was a lovely atmosphere . . . they tried to make everybody happy, even the very ill patients . . .'. Experience of nursing at St Luke's, *c.* 1950. (*BHRU transcript no. H0094*)

While demolition of buildings between Hall Ings, Swaine Street and Colliergate was taking place, this old prison was discovered. It was the old Bradford lock-up which was attached to the Station House between 1836 and 1873. The Station House was used by the commissioners who looked after Bradford's affairs before the Council came into being. It was also home to the Superintendent of the Night Watchmen, who helped keep law and order before policemen were introduced. The lock-up, presumably unused since 1873, certainly looks escape-proof. The site where this was discovered is now home to Central House and the Broadway retail area. (*Bradford Libraries*)

The vast open bowl that is Odsal Stadium has been the venue for many sports other than Rugby League over the years. The Bradford Dukes speedway team raced there for many years, stock car meetings were held in the 1980s, and following the Valley Parade disaster of 1985, Bradford City used Odsal as its home for nearly two years. Yet another sport is seen here, a show-jumping event in the 1950s. Over recent years, various attempts to develop Odsal into a super stadium have so far come to nothing. (*Bradford Libraries*)

Bradford Beck, exposed during work in the Charles Street area, late 1950s. Many of the younger generations of Bradfordians are unaware that there is a stream running under the city centre! (*Bradford Libraries*)

The 1960s and 1970s

Memorial statue to Richard Oastler, Rawson Square, *c.* 1960. Oastler, known as the 'Factory King', championed the cause of children working long hours in often appalling conditions in the textile mills. He eventually succeeded in having the Ten Hours Act passed in 1847. The statue was moved to its current location in Northgate in 1968. (*Bradford Libraries*)

The Broadway area, June 1960. Construction work is well under way on the Broadway, Market Street and Forster Square blocks, with traffic seeming to flow effortlessly through the middle of the building site. (*Mabel Bruce*)

Broadway, with C&A in the background and the ABC cinema to the right, mid-1960s. It seems amazing nowadays to see city centre car parking in areas which have long been pedestrianised. (*Mabel Bruce*)

Broadway precinct, opened in April 1971. (*Jack Booth*)

Development in Hall Ings, mid-1960s. The NCP car park dominates the right of the picture. The open space on the corner of Hall Ings and Bridge Street is the site of the Norfolk Gardens (Hilton) Hotel. The building from which the photograph was taken was demolished to make way for the Magistrates' Courts. (*Bradford Council*)

A skateboarder's paradise! The new walkway taking shape over Hall Ings, between Norfolk Gardens and the Interchange, 1977. (*Jack Booth*)

Tyrrel Street, looking towards Bridge Street, May 1973. In the foreground the site for Provincial House is being cleared, while to the right stand the doomed Mechanics' Institute Buildings. This area now forms part of Centenary Square. (*Jack Booth*)

Redevelopment on the site of Town Hall Square and the Tyrls, January 1966. (*Mabel Bruce*)

The library at Darley Street finally closed its doors at 6 p.m. on Saturday 8 April 1967. Gone are the polished dark wood, high bookshelves, ladders and one reported habit of the Lending Librarian, Norman Hill, of sneaking his pet dachshund into the library on Wednesday afternoons when it was closed to the public. (*Mabel Bruce*)

Foundation work being carried out for the construction of the new Central Library, November 1964. The eight-storey building was opened in 1967 and at the time was the largest library in Europe. (*Bradford Libraries*)

Hall Ings, 1969. The new inner ring road was still under construction. Note the recently built Central Library to the left. The group of old buildings in the centre was demolished to make way for the police station and magistrates' courts. (*Bradford Council*)

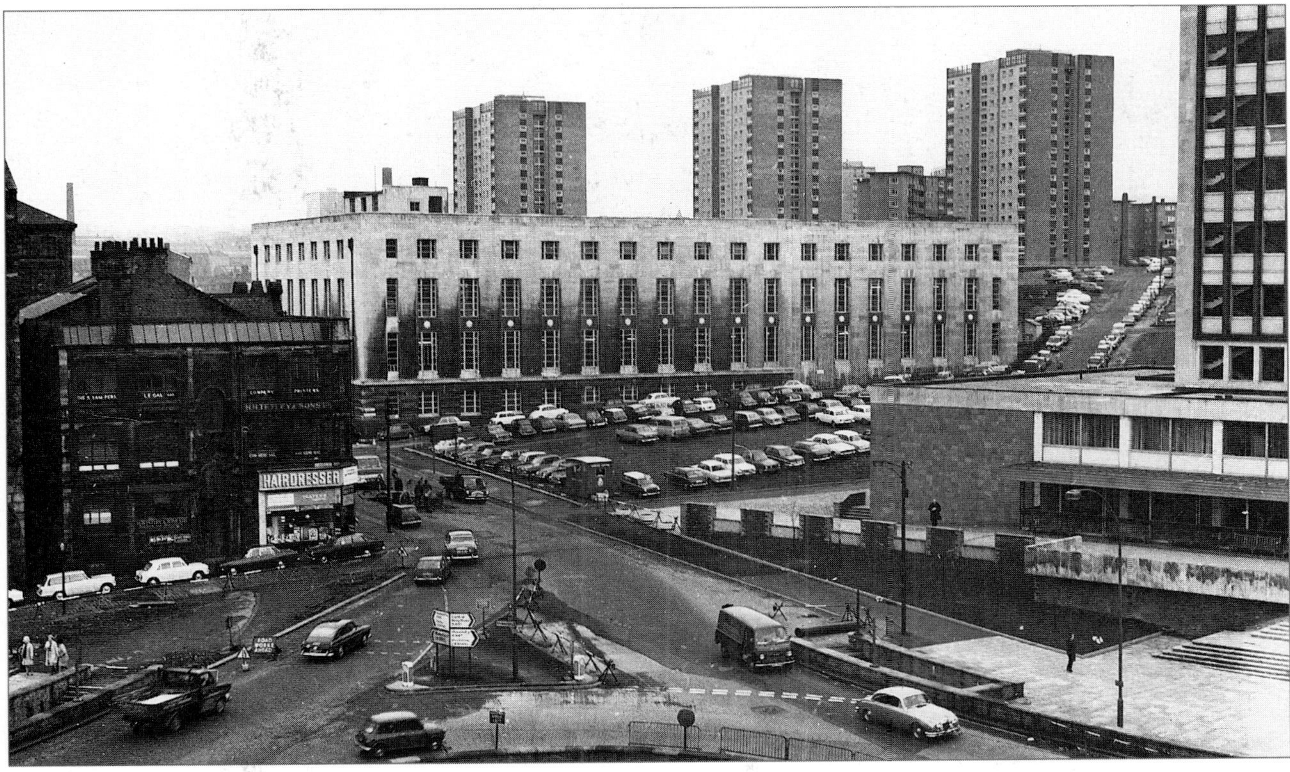

Jacob's Well roundabout, showing the new Central Library to the right. The car park to the left of the library is now occupied by Mercury House. The block of buildings to the left was demolished as part of the Manchester Road widening scheme, and the Jacob's Well offices of the Council built there. (*Bradford Council*)

The Provincial Building Society office block under construction, *c.* 1973. The building dominates the City Hall area and its future has recently been at the centre of intense debate, with arguments for and against its demolition. The once familiar sight of a lorry laden with bales of wool can be seen at the bottom of Thornton Road. (*Bradford Council*)

Prince's Way, Bradford's inner ring road, *c.* 1976. The new police station is clearly visible on the right, along with the Provincial Building Society (later Abbey National) HQ. The older buildings of the Alhambra theatre and Odeon cinema are on the left. (*Bradford Libraries*)

The interior of Adolphus Street goods station, 1970. This was one of the first stations in Bradford, opening to passengers in 1854. When the Exchange station opened thirteen years later, Adolphus Street became a goods station. The bulldozers finally moved in in 1970. (*Jack Booth*)

Cheapside turning circle, 1963. Two trolleybuses wait to enter Market Street while more early '60s architecture springs up to dominate the city centre. (*Mabel Bruce*)

The junction of Hall Ings and Nelson Street, May 1969. The large open space behind the main buildings is now the site of Bradford Interchange Bus Station, while the building on the left was demolished to make way for Metrochange House. (*Bradford Council*)

The new Transport Interchange starts to take shape. This picture was taken on 13 September 1975, half-way through the £17 million scheme. The Interchange, which brought together bus and train stations, was hailed as a European showpiece when it opened. (*Jack Booth*)

Swan Arcade, *c.* 1960. At the beginning of the century this arcade was used by mill owners for their offices, at one of which J.B. Priestley worked. Later its role was that of a shopping centre until its demolition in the 1960s. Many still miss the ornate architecture which Priestley so affectionately described in *Margin Released*. (*Bradford Libraries*)

John Street Market, main entrance, 1971. John Street open market was redeveloped in the early 1960s to include an arched roof, shops and offices and car parking facilities. Although the main body of the market was destroyed by fire in 1977, the main entrance to its replacement remains virtually the same today. (*Bradford Libraries*)

Kirkgate Market, 1967. This was thought by many to be one of the finest market halls in the country, containing over one hundred and thirty-six stalls and fifty-two shops, open daily for the sale of a variety of goods. The exterior shops fronted on two main shopping streets, Darley Street and Kirkgate. (*Bradford Libraries*)

The interior of Kirkgate Market, 1973. Despite protests, the market was demolished in this year. It was once described by John Betjeman as being 'part of the heart of Bradford'. Many Bradfordians mourned its passing. It was replaced by a larger market and modern shopping complex, the Kirkgate Centre. (*Jack Booth*)

Wardley Centre, 1969. Built in the early '60s to house a bingo hall, ice skating rink, library, casino, entertainments and offices, some used by Bradford University, the front part of the building was to house a new Prince's Theatre, but this part of the development never came off. It was known as Bradford's 'white elephant' until plans to make it into a national photographic museum came into being. The National Museum of Photography, Film and Television opened in 1983 and the rest, as they say, is history. (*Bradford Council*)

The ABC Triple cinema, Broadway, 1970s. Once this was the popular Ritz cinema which was opened in 1939 with white tie and tails manager and resident organist. The ABC 1, which seated 732, opened in 1974 with *Blazing Saddles*. The building's other two self-contained cinemas were opened later that year and ran *Man About the House* and *Murder on the Orient Express* to full houses, despite the current recession. Having more than one screen in one building meant films could run for longer periods and earn more money. (*Bradford Libraries*)

Bradford Park Avenue, *c.* 1974. After Park Avenue were voted out of the Football League in 1970, they played three seasons at their beloved ground before being forced to move to Valley Parade. This photograph shows the steady decline of the stands. All that remains of the ground today are a few walls and a slope to show where the terraces once stood. (*Arthur Birdsall*)

Grass grows over the terraces at Park Avenue, *c.* 1974. In its day the stadium was regarded as the better of the two league grounds in Bradford, both in terms of facilities and location. In fact Bradford City FC considered moving there on more than one occasion. (*Arthur Birdsall*)

The Richard Dunn Sports Centre rises above its surroundings, 1977. The centre, costing £3.5 million, was named after the Bradford-born boxer who in 1976 fought Muhammad Ali for the world title. Ironically, between 1975 and 1977 Richard Dunn worked as a scaffolder on the building which was to bear his name. (*Jack Booth*)

Bradford's Unitarian Chapel at the side of City Hall, Chapel Lane, was demolished in 1969. It had a tradition of scholarly ministers. A new church was opened in Russell Street, Little Horton, in 1971. (*Bradford Libraries*)

One of Bradford's first mosques opened in Southfield Square, off Lumb Lane. The Jamiyat Tabligh-Ul-Islam (preaching of Islam) was established in May 1963. (*Bradford Libraries*)

The 'famous', but little seen Bradford Beck, *c.* 1973. Here it is running alongside Canal Road, near the junction with Gaisby Lane, having flowed under the city centre. (*Bradford Libraries*)

A city centre view of Bradford Beck, exposed during workings, this time at Thornton Road. The beck flows through the centre of Bradford, following the course of Thornton Road, passing under Godwin Street and Aldermanbury, the bottom of Ivegate (where Ive Bridge once stood) before turning sharply near Bridge Street and heading for the River Aire, three miles away. (*Jack Booth*)

Church Bank, with Bradford Cathedral just visible on the left and the grand warehouses of Little Germany to the right, 1964. At the bottom of the picture work on the new subways is being carried out. (*Bradford Libraries*)

Pedestrianisation work taking place at the junction of Westgate and Godwin Street, 1973. (*Jack Booth*)

Smile Please! Mabel Bruce was co-founder of the Bradford Camera Club in the 1930s. She undertook the Bradford Photographic Survey in the 1960s. Here she can be seen at work in the city centre with Mr N. Stow. This shot was taken on Market Street. (*Bradford Libraries*)

Norfolk Street/Bridge Street, 1963. The buildings to the left, known as Snowden's Corner, were pulled down later that year, and replaced with the Norfolk Gardens. It seems strange nowadays that the ornate City Hall was once almost surrounded by other, less impressive buildings. (*Bradford Council*)

Beacon Road, winter 1978–9. On 19 January more than twenty-four hours of non-stop snow brought chaos to the roads and left hundreds of people in outlying areas stranded in their homes. Many more had to walk home from work. (*Jack Booth*)

Princess Anne arrives in Bradford city centre on the evening of 22 June 1977, after a Jubilee Tour of the district which took in Ilkley, Keighley, Saltaire and Bradford. (*Bradford Libraries*)

The Lord Mayor, Councillor Paul Hockney (brother of artist David), greets Princess Anne outside City Hall prior to a civic dinner. Later in the evening, a Gala Show was staged at the Alhambra Theatre. (*Bradford Libraries*)

Modern Bradford

Bridge Street, looking down from Bradford Interchange, *c.* 1987. The scene has not changed at all since, although fashions and buses obviously have! The Metro Travel logo was replaced by a more modern design in 1988. (*BHRU*)

The grand interior of the Wool Exchange, a Grade I listed building. It was completed in 1867 and symbolised the wealth and importance Bradford had gained by the mid-nineteenth century, through its wool trade. After its greatest era, it fell into decline and was bought by Bradford Council in 1968, in order to save it from demolition. This photograph, from 1986, shows that trading continued, with regular flea markets and antique fairs. The Exchange now houses a Waterstone's bookshop. (*BHRU*)

Stalls at a Tuesday Market, Wool Exchange, 1986. (*BHRU*)

The new glass frontage of the Wool Exchange, 2000. This scene is taken from Piece Hall Yard and Waterstone's can be clearly seen, along with Starbuck's Coffee Shop upstairs. (*Gina Szekely*)

Mr Napoleon Puc, Slavia Stores, 1986. Many immigrants from Eastern Europe missed the tastes of their homeland. Some established delicatessens and began to import foods such as salami. In 1991 this shop had been a traditional European delicatessen in Bradford for 28 years and won Delicatessen of the Year award for the north-east. (*BHRU*)

F.M. Rimmington and Sons, Chemists, Bridge Street, 1999. This shop has been a familiar sight in Bradford since the 1870s. The business was started in the 1840s by Felix Marsh Rimmington, who had premises in nearby Ivegate. (*Bob Duckett*)

Vicar Lane car park, 1988. This is the site of the old Exchange station. To the left is Drake Street, showing part of St George's Hall and the *Telegraph and Argus* buildings. The new Law Courts were built opposite here and opened in 1993. The rest of the site is still vacant although plans are afoot to build a new multiplex cinema bowling alley, restaurants and leisure facilities there. (*Bradford Libraries*)

Bradford Law Courts, 2000. The £14 million complex opened opposite the Quality Victoria Hotel in 1993. The buildings have been compared to Shakespeare's Globe Theatre. The public square opposite contains a sculpture commemorating the famous Bradford composer, Frederick Delius. The 'leaf' sculpture is meant to symbolize his love of nature. He was born in Claremont in 1863 and died in 1934. The square provides a haven of peace in a bustling city. (*Pete Walker*)

Zetland Mill, Wharf Street, Bradford, 1986. The mill, seen here being demolished, was the scene of a great disaster in 1924. On Thursday 10 January, the top floor of the mill collapsed, crashing down on to the second floor, which in turn crashed down on to the first floor, ground floor and basement. Four people died and twenty-one were injured. Considering the size of the collapse, and the fact that around fifty people were working there at the time, these casualty figures were, thankfully, quite low. (*BHRU*)

The front of the Alhambra theatre, with Morley Street running up from the left and Great Horton Road on the right, 1986. The Alhambra opened on 18 March 1914 and has been graced by many stars, from Laurel and Hardy to Vesta Tilley. It is still famed for its pantomimes among other productions, as well as staging touring West End musicals. Note the Alexandra Hotel up Great Horton Road. This has now been demolished, with plans to build Britain's first 'peace museum' there. The Empire Music Hall behind the hotel in 1899 showcased Charlie Chaplin in 1906. (*BHRU*)

The modern façade of the National Museum of Photography, Film and Television, May 2000. The new glass frontage was added in 1999, as the museum closed for a revamp to bring it into the twenty-first century. The £16 million refurbishment meant that many of the exhibits had to be moved and kept in storage at the nearby Black Dyke Mills in Queensbury. The new digital galleries and exhibition space will help the NMPFT keep its place as one of the most visited museums outside London. (*Mick Birdsall*)

In the early 1960s there were few Asian restaurants in Bradford. The Karachi on Neal Street, seen here in May 2000, and the Sweet Centre on Lumb Lane are two that have survived and remained popular. At first they catered for the immigrant population, but gradually Bradfordians began to realise that they liked the taste of this 'new' spicy food. The industry grew rapidly until Bradford came to be regarded as the Curry Capital of Britain, with over one hundred establishments in the city, ranging from busy cafés (like the Karachi) to sumptuous restaurants. (*Pete Walker*)

Another of Bradford's more famous names, the Mumtaz restaurant on Great Horton Road sells its curries to top stores such as Harrods, and even has franchises in airports. There are plans to extend the restaurant to make it the largest Asian restaurant in Europe. (*Gina Szekely*)

One of Bradford's best-known restaurants is the Bombay Brasserie. Located in a former Presbyterian chapel on Simes Street, it is well known for its quality food and surroundings. Originally St Andrew's Presbyterian Chapel, built in 1849, it was popular with Bradford's Scottish community and earned itself the nickname 'The Scotch Church'. (*Gina Szekely*)

The former chapel which houses the Bombay Brasserie is also home to a nursery. (*Gina Szekely*)

Laying the foundation stone for the new mosque, off Drewton Road, 1986. The mosque is set to be the largest in Britain and the dome is based on that of a mosque in Istanbul. (*BHRU*)

Drewton Road Mosque, June 2000. These are preparations for a march to celebrate the holy birthday of the Holy Prophet of Islam, Mohammed. (*Gina Szekely*)

Drewton Road Mosque, June 2000. (*Gina Szekely*)

Bombay Stores, Shearbridge Road, May 2000: an Aladdin's Cave of eastern wares, ranging from fabrics to crafts, cookware to musical instruments. The store opened in 1967 on Great Horton Road and moved to its current premises in 1983. The business has gone from strength to strength and attracts people from all over the country. Coach parties are not an uncommon sight. (*Gina Szekely*)

Viraj Saree Centre, Leeds Road, 1999. This is one of the many shops in Bradford selling sarees and a range of printed and plain satin, crêpe, cotton, silk, lamé, net and velvet in a myriad of colours. (*Bob Duckett*)

Statue of author and playwright J.B. Priestley, in front of the National Museum of Photography, 1999. Priestley seems to be looking out over his beloved Bradford, of which he was made a freeman. He is depicted wearing his favourite overcoat, which he kept for twenty years. (*Bob Duckett*)

The 3-metre high 'buried bulb', situated in Bradford's new Forster Square Retail Park, May 2000. Designed by Andy Hazell, it is made of stainless steel, surrounded by neon illuminated glass troughs and yellow shafts of light. It is one of a number of 'controversial' works of art and sculpture located throughout the city centre. (*Gina Szekely*)

A corner of 'old Bradford', tucked away behind 1960s Cheapside. The original façade of the Midland Railway station (Forster Square) and the imposing Midland Hotel, June 1997. (*Bob Duckett*)

Bank Street, looking down towards Hustlergate, 1999. Note the street bunting in place ready for the Bradford Festival. The Virgin Megastore is located in part of the former Brown Muffs store. When this closed in 1994, it was refurbished and let in smaller units. These are now occupied by famous high street names. (*Gina Szekely*)

A general view of Bradford city centre from Undercliffe Cemetery, 1986. Developments from the 1960s and '70s have all but taken over the city centre, and most of the fine Victorian buildings which still survive are hidden from view. (*BHRU*)

The new frontage of Bradford Interchange. The whole concourse was modernised and the new canopy added in 1996. Work is currently under way to refurbish the whole of the bus station. The landmark glass roof has already gone and will be replaced by a large concourse with bus stands based around it. Shops and cafés will be provided to cater for the 24,000 people who use the Interchange every day. (*Bob Duckett*)

Bradford Forster Square station, June 2000. The £33 million station was opened in 1990 to replace the rundown original. Trains from the 'electrified' station now serve Ilkley, Shipley, Keighley, Skipton and Leeds. There is also an Intercity service to London. Next to the station are the new Inland Revenue offices. (*Pete Walker*)

Richmond Building, Bradford University, 1999. The university received its Royal Charter in 1966. It grew out of Bradford Institute of Technology, which was formed in the 1860s. The university's strengths lie in the fields of Applied Science and Engineering, but it also provides many unique courses such as Peace Studies. In 1999 there were around 7,000 students enrolled there. (*Bob Duckett*)

Great Horton Road, looking down towards the city centre, 1999. To the left is the grand architecture of Bradford College's old building. This stretch of Great Horton Road is the site of Bradford's 'education precinct', home to the university and college. (*Bob Duckett*)

JAGUAR

Bradford City players celebrate the club's promotion to the Premiership, May 1999. The Bantams secured top-flight football for the first time in 77 years with a thrilling 3–2 victory at Wolverhampton. This photograph was taken on 13 May after a celebration match against a side put together by former player John Hendrie. (*Andy Bell*)

Valley Parade, home of Bradford City FC, May 2000. The giant Kop Stand towers over the houses on Rock Terrace. The transformation of the stadium started with the building of the Midland Road Stand, visible to the left of the photograph, which opened in 1996. When the new main stand opens during the 2000/2001 season, the ground will be barely recognisable from the Valley Parade which was rebuilt following the tragic fire of May 1985. (*Pete Walker*)

Throughout the 1990s Bradford Festival has gained a growing reputation as one of Britain's brightest and best summer festivals. Here, in 1992, the Nachda Punjab Dancers perform on Bank Street at the side of the Wool Exchange. (*Tim Smith, Bradford Festival*)

An Asian dancing troupe entertaining the crowds at the 1993 festival. Street performances are one of the most popular aspects of the festival, with acts from all over Britain and abroad. (*Tim Smith, Bradford Festival*)

No chauffeur required! Lord Mayor Barry Thorne hitches a lift on board a decorated elephant during a parade at the 1992 festival. (*Tim Smith, Bradford Festival*)

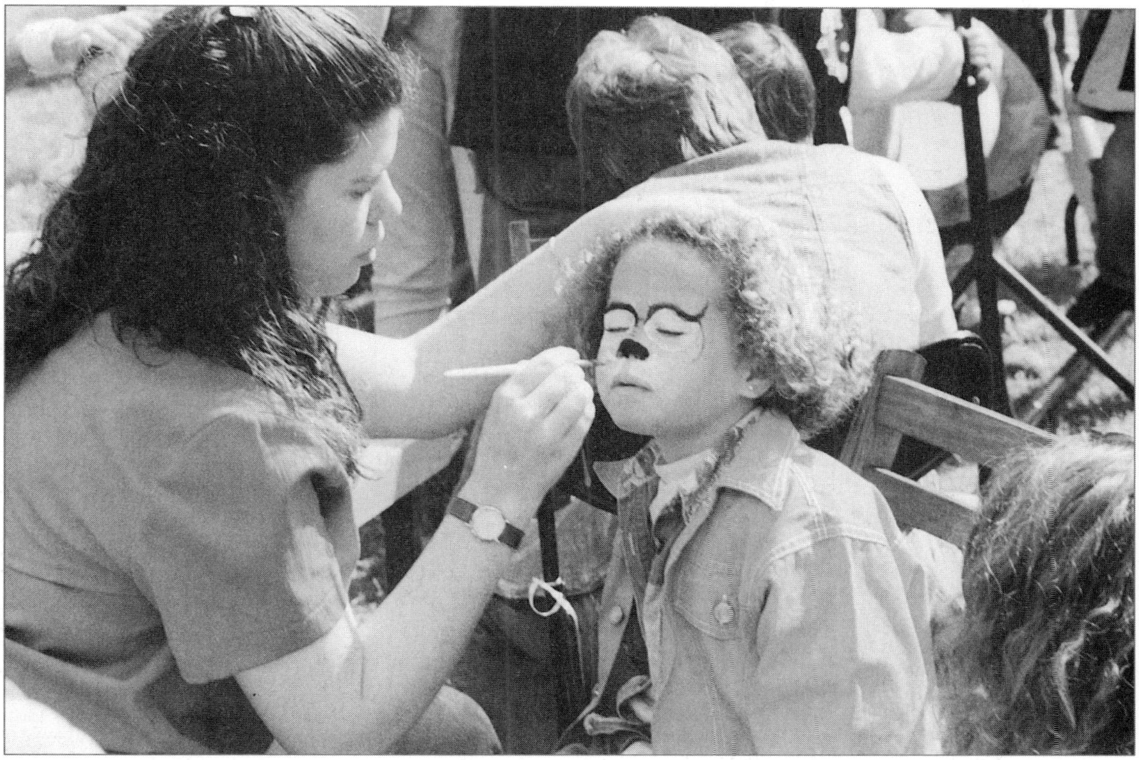

Face painting fun at the Mela, Lister Park, 1996. (*Maurice Manktelow*)

The crowd in a happy mood at the 1998 Mela. The Mela is the highlight of every Bradford Festival. It brings together a myriad of local, national and international artists as well as boasting bazaars, a funfair and stalls selling a huge range of international cuisines. (*Tim Smith, Bradford Festival*)

Bradford Festival 1998
GUINNESS FESTIVAL FLING
GUINNESS

The Guinness Festival Fling, Centenary Square. Bradford folk are enjoying the craic at this three-day Celtic music event which kicked off the 1998 festival. Centenary Square, opened in 1996, is a focal point for events in the city centre. (*Tim Smith, Bradford Festival*)

All smiles at the Mela, 1996. (*Tim Smith, Bradford Festival*)

Acknowledgements

This book has only been made possible by the kind help of many different people and organisations. There are too many to mention here but our special thanks must go to: all the staff in the Reference and Local Studies department of Bradford Central Library for their usual help and assistance, with a special thank-you to Bob Duckett and Carol Greenwood; Bradford Heritage Recording Unit; the staff at Bradford Festival offices; House of Fraser; Mr and Mrs Booth for their permission to use the photographs of the late Jack Booth; the late Mabel Bruce; Maurice and Pam Manktelow, Andy Bell and Terry Cranmer; and the late Arthur Birdsall. Thanks also to all our families for their help and support.

Cock & Bottle, Barkerend Road, 1999. One of the city's most famous pubs, the Cock & Bottle became Britain's first Christian pub when it was taken over by the Bradford Christian Pub Consortium in June 1999. (*Bob Duckett*)

National & Provincial